Hard-Hat Productivity:
The 9 Critical Factors for
Maximizing Profits

Hard-Hat Productivity: The 9 Critical Factors for Maximizing Profits

Norb Slowikowski

iUniverse, Inc.

New York Lincoln Shanghai

Hard-Hat Productivity: The 9 Critical Factors for Maximizing Profits

iUniverse books may be ordered through booksellers or by contacting:

iUniverse
2021 Pine Lake Road, Suite 100
Lincoln, NE 68512
www.iuniverse.com
1-800-Authors (1-800-288-4677)

ISBN-13: 978-0-595-39784-6
ISBN-10: 0-595-39784-0

Printed in the United States of America

Contents

Introduction vii

Critical Factor #1 Embarking on a Journey to Excellence 1

Critical Factor #2 The Hard-Hat Basics 5

Critical Factor #3 Building Teamwork 25

Critical Factor #4 Meeting the Leadership Challenge 41

Critical Factor #5 Organization & Alignment. 53

Critical Factor #6 Motivation 73

Critical Factor #7 The Customer 83

Critical Factor #8 Developing People 95

Critical Factor #9 Managing Change 105

Addendum Productivity Assessment Indicator 111

Introduction

For a guy who started out with next-to-no knowledge of the construction industry, it's ironic to be writing a book entitled "Hard-Hat Productivity." But sometimes life takes you in interesting and unforeseen directions.

In 1980, I was a fledgling owner of my management consultant company, Slowikowski & Associates. After years of work in the corporate environment of McDonald's, I changed paths to start my own business. Most of my clients were in the business and corporate arena and I was working to build a solid foundation in self-employment. Then along came an opportunity in disguise.

I was invited to give a luncheon speech for a group on the subject of Productivity. Although I wasn't getting paid for the event, I looked at it as a good opportunity to get in front of people and market my services to whoever would listen. Luckily for me, someone was listening.

Upon completion of the luncheon, an individual approached me and said he really enjoyed the presentation. He then asked me if I knew anything about the field of construction. When I replied, "No", he told me that he was the Chairman of the Education Committee for a Chicago based Construction Association. He went on to say that he was looking for someone to develop a training program for Foremen and Superintendents in the area of management skills. Unbeknownst to me, my speech focused on several issues the construction industry faces on a regular basis.

Although flattered, I wasn't quite sure that I should get involved in an industry I knew nothing about. But after about a month or so, curiosity got the best of me. I felt that if I did the proper research, I might be able to make something of this while helping out a business in need. I decided to arrange a meeting to get into the details of what he was looking for. After the meeting, I came up with a system that would result in the formation of a training program.

To ensure that the program represented the specific needs of the user, I set aside two years for an adequate research period. This would allow me numerous job site visits and one-on-one discussion with Foremen across all trades. I wanted to get to the heart of problems on the job site while identifying skills needed to effectively cope with these obstacles. I would also spend time in discussion with Owners, Project Managers, Superintendents, Estimators and Support Staff personnel to get their views on what skills they thought Foremen needed to become more productive and effective. I knew that if I immersed myself in the world of construction, I could develop the training program.

Through this system of learning, I developed a training program entitled *Dynamics of Supervision*. The program included six 3-hour modules that dealt with the management and leadership skills needed to effectively manage a project and motivate workers on the job. Specific focus was placed on the transition from Journeyman to Foreman with an emphasis on the key skills of planning, organizing, directing, controlling and leadership. The *Supervision* program was launched in 1984 and is still offered today. Through the years I've repeated the process for dozens of companies. I've been able to incorporate new lessons and customize the program to fit the needs of each and every contractor.

In the end, the challenge of jumping into the construction industry was about turning an opportunity into a reality. I knew that if I had sufficient knowledge of the industry, I could use the information I gathered as a resource to help contractors improve job site productivity. The program was subsequently developed and field-tested and has been consistently honed to fit the changing needs of the industry. The new direction put me on track for a rewarding career that would provide a viable service to more than 200 construction companies in the US & Canada. Through continuing research and "hands-on" involvement with all of the players in the construction process, I continue to identify and meet the needs of everyone involved.

All the hard work through the years led to the culmination of the *Productivity Improvement Process*, the process that brought along the inspiration to write this book. It is through this process that I discovered the Nine Critical Factors for improving job site productivity and employee effectiveness at all levels of a construction company.

The book clearly and directly describes how to improve overall job productivity and organizational effectiveness by building a strong, unified team that supports the job site team.

This is a "Journey to Excellence" based on four Building Blocks:

- Focus
- Climate
- Alignment
- Deployment

These blocks are put in place through effective Management, Leadership and Teamwork at all levels of the organization. This is the blueprint for maximizing profits—which is ultimately the name of the game.

Let's get started!

Critical Factor #1

Embarking on a Journey to Excellence

- **Defininition of Excellence**
- **Requirements for Achieving Excellence**
- **Clarifying and Delivering Values**
- **Build Commitment**
- **Build Trustworthy Leadership**

Embarking on a Journey to Excellence

Definition of Excellence

1. Striving for perfection.

2. Painstaking attention to details.

3. Endless work.

4. Doing your best.

5. Working smarter, not harder.

6. Embracing change.

Requirements for Achieving Excellence

Build Trust: The word trust is derived from the German word "trost," which suggests comfort. Trust is defined as belief that those on whom we depend will meet our expectations of them.

Three concepts are imperative for building trust:

1. People's performance in fulfilling their obligations and commitments. They must have clearly defined expectations to achieve the desired results.

2. Acting with integrity, honesty in one's words, and consistency in one's actions. Our most important expecations in a given situation must be fulfilled.

3. Demonstrating concern for others. We trust those who care about us. We trust those whom we believe understand our concerns and will act in a way that meets or at least does not conflict with our needs. It has a lot to do with support from above.

Clarifying & Delivering Values

<u>Value</u>: A principle, standard, or quality considered inherently worthwhile or desirable. The root is the Latin, "valor," which means strength. Values are sources of strength because they give people the power to take action.

Values have the following characteristics:

- Help organize lives.
- The bedrock of corporate culture.
- Define the way people actually do things in an organization.
- Spur us on to great achievements.
- Motivate people to work together.
- Delivered to customers and employees through behavior.
- Come alive when they are expressed in behaviors.

It is important to clarify the organization's values and align each of them with specific behaviors that become commitments for action. The values become your business ethic that should never be compromised.

Build Commitment

<u>Commitment</u>: People have a sense of doing meaningful work. They have a clear vision about where they are going that is largely in line with their basic values, allowing them to be involved and motivated in their work.

We need to build a work climate where employees are empowered to "want" to do their best. If you want more from your people, give them more of what they value which includes:

- Clearly defined expectations and standards of performance.
- Treat them with dignity and respect.
- Offer them jobs with meaning.
- Let them know what's going on. Share information.

- Involve them in decision-making.
- Offer them opportunities to control their own work.
- Provide support when they face difficulties.
- Provide opportunities for growth and development.

Build Trustworthy Leadership

Since trust is built primarily on actions rather than pronouncements, leaders need to act in ways that clearly demonstrate their commitment to achieving results, acting with integrity, and demonstrating genuine concern for others. To meet these requirements, the leader must do the following:

- Set high performance standards, be personally accountable for achieving them, and hold others to the same standard.
- Be completely honest with everyone in the organization.
- Demonstrate the 10 Leader Behaviors every day.
  1. Involvement
  2. Collaboration
  3. Accessibility
  4. Visibility
  5. Encourage Feedback
  6. Listening
  7. Positive Reinforcement
  8. Coaching
  9. Taking Action
  10. Accountability
- Make contact with people to understand what's going on in their world.
- Take effective action to meet customer's expectations.

Critical Factor #2

The Hard-Hat Basics

- Defining Hard-Hat Productivity
- Hart-Hat FAQ: Common Contractor Questions
- Creating Everyday Productivity on the Job
- Clarifying the Foreman's Role
- Strengthening the Project Manager/Foreman Partnership
- Removing the Hidden Barriers to Productivity

Defining Hard-Hat Productivity

To be successful is to be productive.

When we filter out all the roadblocks and unnecessary diversions, we are left with the ingredient that makes great companies tick: Productivity.

Productivity is the effective utilization of resources to achieve the quantity and quality of output within specific time frames. When you break it down, productivity is defined by two main elements:

What is *effective*: do the right things (process)
What is *efficient*: do things right (quality)

In short, if the company can be effective and efficient, they will be productive.

There are seven resources required for optimizing productivity:

- Tools
- Equipment
- Material
- Manpower
- Information
- Training
- Support

To be effective and efficient, the Foreman on the job site needs all seven resources. If one of these is lacking, the job site team will not perform at an optimum level.

It takes a special person to be an effective Foreman. A combination of knowledge, experience and skills is necessary to be the "go-to guy" on the job site. Some of the basic abilities needed are:

- Understand the Scope of Work, the Quality Specs for the job and Contractual Requirements.

- Be technically competent and know how to do your job.

- Establish a positive work climate so that people want to come to work everyday and do their best work.

- Effective utilization of tools, equipment, material and people.

- Embrace change.

- Plan, organize, direct, control and lead.

- Set production goals with the crew.

- Monitor and assess the quality of workmanship and make corrections as required.

- Establish accountability.

- Be a coach and not a critic.

Hard-Hat FAQ—Common Contractor Questions

In my work with contractors around the country, I've been asked a lot of questions about people management, leadership and the skills field supervisors need to be more effective on the job. With that in mind, here are the most Frequently Asked Questions (FAQ) along with my ideas as to why they're important for achieving optimum productivity on the job site.

Question: What is the main objective that a contractor should strive for in trying to improve productivity in a company?

I'd have to say, "establish a positive work climate." You can't possibly motivate an individual with the same techniques that worked ten or more years ago.

Most contractors are aware of this principle but I will recite it anyway. I call it the "lengthening shadow approach." As a contractor goes, so goes his organization. If a contractor is uptight, angry, hostile and disrespectful, the company will soon take on that personality. Everyone is a lengthening shadow of the leader.

For that reason, a contractor should look at his foremen and superintendents as key assets to success. If a contractor is a positive and fair individual, he'll spot that Foreman who's out of tune with the company culture and will do something about it in a positive way—simply using straight talk and listening.

Establishing a positive climate also requires positive reinforcement for a job well done—rewards for top performers, involving field supervisors in the decision-making process and encouraging them to ask for help right away when they encounter a problem they don't know how to handle. This requires upper management to adopt a "let's fix it" attitude, instead of blaming others when problems occur.

Question: How can an owner stay in touch with all levels of his organization and still run the business effectively?

Actually, it isn't all that hard to do. I call it the MBWA approach—Manage by Walking Around.

A contractor should schedule time to visit the job site and find out what's going on. Most contractors practice this principle anyway. It's just good business sense.

But don't restrict your fact-finding to job progress. Talk to and especially listen to your people. Don't be so certain that your Foremen and Supervisors will automatically tell you they're having problems. You need to encourage feedback without repercussions attached.

Let your people know that you're interested in them and in their work. Ask them if you can help in any way. Give some credit where credit is due. Nothing is more motivating than for the boss to show appreciation. It's amazing what that does for people and there's no cost attached to it.

Question: Are there any "must-do's" that owners should carry out when they visit the job site?

People today want three things. First, they want to feel involved and be a part of the team. Second, they want sincere appreciation for a job well done. Third, they want the feeling that you'll support them when they're facing difficulty, that when an obstacle occurs, you'll take action to assist them or help them remove it.

The old excuse that good employees don't need positive feedback because they know when they're doing well is archaic thinking that doesn't match with what employees want.

Question: What's a good rule to apply when an owner spots a problem situation on the job site?

Remember, people typically don't deliberately foul things up, so watch out for overreacting and placing blame. Instead, keep your focus on the problem and what caused it. You should involve the Foreman in the solution since he's the one in charge.

When everyone focuses on a problem, a sense of achievement and belonging occurs. Follow these simple rules to make sure the process is successful:

- Attack the problems, not the people.
- Involve key people in the solution.
- Maintain emotional control.
- Be a coach.

Question: What are the key elements of effective job site supervision?

First of all, the job site supervisor must be able to identify the barriers to productivity and eliminate them. He must identify the underlying causes and avoid treating the symptoms.

The first step is to specifically identify the problem. Is it poor morale? Too much waiting? Poor planning? Logistics? Ineffective scheduling? Lack of support from the office? Late deliver of materials? A problem that is specifically identified is already half-solved.

The second key element is listening. Do we really tune in and understand what people are saying? Do we hear people out before reacting? Do we repeat back to people what our understanding of the message is? Do we give people one-on-one quality listening time on a periodic basis? Do we understand what people expect of us? Do we encourage and listen to suggestions from the field? Remember, if someone is not listening, communication fails.

The third element is motivating people. Knowing what makes people tick is knowing their driving force. It's satisfying their needs and wants, which includes the following:

- Sincere appreciation for a job well done.

- Involving them in decision-making.

- Supporting them when the going gets tough.

- Letting them know how they're doing and coaching them when improvement is needed.

- Giving them all the information they need to do their job effectively. For example, labor budget, scope or work, blueprints, shop drawings, addendums, copy of the contract, adequate tools and equipment, etc.

- Treating them as key members of the team.

Everything we've talked about in this section can be easily summed up in the following:

"Let your people on the job site know what the goals are and involve them in developing an Action Plan to achieve the desired results. Let them help you solve problems. Let them create a sense of "team" so that everyone is moving toward the same goal—improving productivity on the job site."

Creating Everyday Productivity on the Job

Improving productivity requires effective leadership and management by the general superintendent and other key players in the process. By implementing these success factors, the following will be enhanced:

- Taking ownership

- Pride of workmanship

- Peak performance

- Job profitability

Conduct Personal Pre Job Planning

The general superintendent should take the time to visit the job once you get the job. He will identify the conditions under which the crew will be expected to work, and will take the time to check out such things as:

- Nature of the work. What specifically will your crew have to do?

- Tools, equipment and material needed to produce quality for specified work.

- Control of manpower and labor. Develop a Staffing Chart, log it daily.

- Other trades you will be working with. How long will it take them to complete their work before our crew gets into the space? Build positive relationships with the other trades, and find out all you can to work together as a team.

- Customer requirements. What are the standards for production, quality, safety, security, equipment, rules etc? Initiate customer contact. Document what you and the customer representatives discuss so you can minimize any conflicts that may arise at a later date. The rules may change as the job progresses.

Communicate Effectively

- Clarify expectations. Make sure your people are clear about their responsibilities and the results they will be held accountable for.

- Identify performance problems and discuss solutions with individuals involved.

- Provide positive feedback when things are going well. People need to hear how they are doing.

- Provide coaching when things aren't going well. Get your people on the right track through your knowledge and experience.

Implement Job Controls

- Review and explain paperwork requirements (time sheets, labor coding, job logs, safety reports, inventory, checklists etc.).

- Conduct a pre-job planning meeting with all key players on the job.

- Conduct weekly job progress meetings and review how well the labor budget is being managed. When the job is over budget, investigate for underlying causes and take action to get back on budget.

- Conduct post job review to identify the positive and negative results. Make it a learning experience.

Implement a Game Plan

- Involve foremen in documenting extra work requests. Get it in writing, be specific and obtain an authorized signature.

- Collaborate on all goals. Discuss what needs to be done and set a time frame for completion as a team.

- Introduce the foreman to the customer and clarify expectations.

- Match the right people with the right skills to do the job. Check the conditions: high work, cramped space, outside/inside work, hot/cold conditions, a solo job.

- Before you leave the job site, let the foreman know the positive things you have observed. Identify the areas that need improvement and develop actions to eliminate the obstacles.
- Track and measure foreman's progress.
- Conduct weekly job progress meetings.
- Keep the lines of communication open. Let the foreman know you want feedback when he runs into a problem. Adopt a solutions-orientation.

Check, Measure & Correct

- Check foreman's performance on labor control, safety, housekeeping, tool and equipment control, quality workmanship, paperwork, customer relations, and communication with project manager and office support staff.
- Listen to any and all suggestions for improving the process.
- Coach and take corrective action. Establish accountability. Celebrate success.

Clarifying the Foreman's Role

An effective Foreman must have the ability to deal with the "soft" and "hard" factors that play a role in making productivity improvement a reality on the job site. The "soft" factors are the management and leadership skills that affect the motivation of the crew. The "hard" factors are quality installation, meeting the schedule, maintaining a safe work environment, documentation, Two-Week Look Ahead Scheduling and tool, equipment, material control.

Managing and Leading Effectively

Soft Factors

Key Management Skills	Key Leadership Skills
-Planning	-Effective Communication
-Organizing	-Motivating Others
-Directing	-Dealing with Different Personality Types
-Controlling	-Establishing a Motivational Climate
	-Resolving Conflict
	-Job Site Disputes
	-Negotiating Effectively
	-Coaching
	-Problem-Solving
	-Building Teamwork

Foremen must become proficient in the following skills areas if they are going to be effective in managing the project and leading the people:

1. They first must have a thorough knowledge and mastery of how to do the work and then provide the proper resources so that their crew can be productive.

2. They must lead by example—by practicing good work habits, they will gain respect and be more likely to instill these admirable qualities in their crew.

3. They must be able to organize, anticipate and solve problems, make decisions, adjust to change, participate in pre-job planning sessions and give comprehensible instructions to their crews before the job starts.

4. They must show care and concern for their employees by helping workers improve when they make mistakes, rather than using criticism when mistakes are made.

5. They should establish a motivational climate on the job site by providing the following key job satisfiers that make employees feel "in" on things:

    • Keeping them informed about what goes on at management meetings.

    • Soliciting input about barriers that impede performance on the job site.

    • Encouraging suggestions and implementing them when they make sense.

Controlling Job Costs

Other than direct control of the workforce, there are other factors which have a substantial bearing on job costs. While going over these factors, keep one thought in mind—each example is laden with potential excuses for why production is not being met. The good foreman eliminates the possibility for excuses. He takes excuses away from himself and his crew.

1. Material Distribution

When materials are delivered to a job, every effort should be made to locate them in a strategic place near the work area. If the crew has to go from one floor to another or from one area to another to get the materials they need, they will lose a tremendous amount of time. Keep materials close to the work area.

2. Material Quantities

The job cost and production are directly related to the amount of material on the job. Constant checking of materials to anticipate shortages is important. If the crew doesn't have the right type or quantity of material with which to do the work, they can be standing around on your time waiting for delivery. Also, remember that if you have too much material on a project, the labor cost of bringing it back to the warehouse can be high, especially if it is on an upper floor and has to be hand carried to your truck. Overstocking is as critical as understocking. The right amount and type of material is directly related to lost time and delivery costs.

3. Quality of Workmanship

Keep your crew quality conscious by continuous self-inspection and quality audits. Do the work right the first time. Repeated call backs and punch list items can be eliminated with a good quality control. Extra trips for repairs and adjustments are expensive headaches. Be sure to follow up and check the work of your crew several times a day. If they're doing quality work, provide positive reinforcement. If they're not, intervene and provide coaching to get them back on the right track.

4. Tools and Equipment

Be sure your crew has the proper tools and equipment to do the job. Keep a watchful eye for crew members who are not using the tools properly. Get involved and explain that it's important to use the tools properly to achieve quality results. Keep your equipment in good repair and gang boxes properly stocked. Pay attention to your company's ordering procedures so that the proper tools and equipment get to the job site when needed.

5. Safety

Constant instruction in safety procedures will eliminate lost time, prevent accidents and lower insurance rates. Insurance rates reflect your company's experience. If your experience is good, your rates will be lower. If bad, rates will increase. Remember that insurance is a big percentage of the labor cost on every job. Lower your costs by being safety conscious. Lower insurance rates lead directly to more work, which provides security for your crew. Make sure your Foreman conducts effective weekly tool box talks.

6. Housekeeping

Be sure your crew has proper equipment for cleaning and rubbish removal. Clear, clean, unobstructed work areas are important to increased productivity and safety. Make necessary arrangements with the customer for trash removal. Maintain good housekeeping for good customer relations.

Strengthening the Project Manager/Foreman Partnership

There are many different aspects that go into the Project Manager/Foreman relationship. If the pathway between these two main components is cluttered with miscommunication and problems, the entire operation consequently suffers. Each party needs to know what makes the other tick. The Project Manager has to take the lead and follow a series of guidelines in order for the partnership to work at an optimum level.

- Review the estimate with the Foreman. How many man-days are in the estimate? Review actual staffing against the estimate. Make adjustments as required. Are there better ways to get the work done? Make sure the customer agrees with the way you want to proceed.

- Make sure that the quality of work meets the customer's requirements. You may want to have the customer review the quality of your work at various stages of the job. Schedule such a meeting in advance.

- Conduct an on-site safety inspection when you go to a job. Walk the job with the Foreman and review what both of you observe. Discuss taking corrective measures where appropriate.

- Check the Foreman's performance on maintaining a clean environment. Review discrepancies and discuss remedial measures. Expect improvement. Provide positive feedback when cleanliness standards are met.

- Make sure that the company issued tools are properly maintained and that the Foremen have the tools they are supposed to have. Review with them the tool requirements as specified for the job.

- Ensure that the Foreman fulfills all paperwork requirements and completes them in a legible, accurate, timely manner.

- Encourage the Foreman to communicate to you any barrier that affects his effectiveness or productivity on the job. Tell him that you can't help him if he doesn't tell you about these barriers. Let him know that it's okay to communicate problems. You are there to help eliminate them. Examples of some barriers are: Late delivery or wrong material sent to a job, broken equipment, lack of support from GC's Supt., irate customers, lack of timely information.

- Remind the Foreman that he is the company's representative on the job. The way he talks, behaves and presents himself to the customer and the other tradesmen is essential for building teamwork on the jobsite. He must provide excellent service to your internal and external customers.

- Make sure you communicate to the Foreman that he will be required at times to order materials that may not be shown on the blueprints. Tell him that you expect him to make those judgments and follow through on such assignments. It's important to communicate with the PM when this becomes necessary.

- Inform the Foreman that it's important to practice positive customer relations with other trades, his own crew and the customer. He needs to be sensitive to the customer's needs, communicate them to the appropriate people and then follow up to see that those needs are met.

- Let the Foreman know that you are extremely interested in any input he has that will improve productivity on the jobsite. If he has suggestions to do things better, you're listening.

- Explain to the Foreman that it's very important that he knows how to read and understand prints and specifications. You may ask the customer's engineer or PM to review these items with you and the Foreman when you are on the jobsite. You may have to provide individual coaching or ask him to attend a training class to improve this essential skill. It should not be overlooked.

- Again, mention to the Foreman that he has to inform the PM anytime something occurs that will hamper productivity or obstruct positive progress on the job. Stay away from any conflict with other people. Communicate the problem to your PM immediately so that remedial action can be taken.

Removing the Hidden Barriers to Productivity

Many times, contractors are unsure about why productivity is down or why there are work delays on the job site. The answers are not that complicated, yet the common causes remain hidden because many times owners are not in tune with what is really happening on a job site. This lack of listening, support and follow-through results in inefficiency and poor morale.

Following are some of the major hidden barriers that have surfaced through extensive discussions with a sampling of superintendents and job site foremen.

Hidden Barrier #1—Negative Work Climate

The missing pieces include the following:

- Foremen do not understand the scope of work. It is rarely explained to them.

- Too much criticizing. You make a mistake and you are sure to hear about it (many times belittled and put down). Little help is given to correct the mistake.

- Too much second-guessing. You make a decision and then your boss comes around and says he would not have done it that way. But when you call for help, everyone is too busy to get involved.

- Too many non-productive activities, caused by late deliveries, lack of instruction and insufficient information.

Hidden Barrier #2—Poor Communication System

The biggest barrier is lack of listening. When you have an idea or a solution to a problem, you cannot find anyone who will take the time to hear you out. You are constantly interrupted and told to follow the boss's way of doing things, even if it doesn't make sense. Basically, input from the field is not encouraged.

Another barrier is the project manager's unfamiliarity with job site conditions. When you try to talk to him/her about a problem, there is little understanding of what you're talking about. Worse, there seems to be little desire on the part of the PM to come out to the job site and find out what is going on. This results in the crew keeping problems to themselves or telling the PM what he wants to hear.

A third barrier that goes under this heading has to do with ineffective job progress meetings. These meetings are generally poorly organized. Without an objective and an agenda, too much room is left for "preaching" and a lack of input. This ends up being a colossal waste of time.

Hidden Barrier #3—Inadequate Tool & Equipment Maintenance and Repair Program

This is a twofold problem. First, the foreman fails to tag defective equipment and identify what is wrong with it. The result is defective equipment being delivered to another job site. Even if the equipment is tagged, there is nobody in the shop qualified to repair it and it's not even sent out for repair. The warehouse supervisor simply stacks the equipment in a corner. This one factor costs the contractor a lot of money, since the foreman does not have operable equipment to do the job.

Hidden Barrier #4—Poor People Practices

Field supervisors identified the following "demotivators" that they consider to impact productivity in an extreme manner.

Lack of Pre-Job Planning. You are told to come to the office to pick up the blueprints for a job that starts tomorrow. Nobody sits down with you to explain the scope of the project you are asked to take on.

Disrespectful treatment. Tired of being yelled at or berated in front of others.

Lack of recognition. Little or no positive feedback when you do something well. You are taken for granted. It would be nice to hear good news once in a while.

Lack of participation in the decision-making process. Office personnel make decisions about job site problems without asking for the foreman's input. Many times wrong decisions are made and we have to live with those decisions with little or no support from our superiors. The decisions are reactive instead of proactive.

So there you have it! Do any of these hidden barriers sound familiar? Before you say, "they don't exist in my organization," may I suggest that you come out of hiding, bring your field supervisors together and listen!

Critical Factor #3

Building Teamwork

- **Creating a Team Mentality**
- **Why Teamwork?**
- **It All Starts with Planning**

Creating a Team Mentality

In the world of business, there is a basic formula used on a day-to-day basis to move the organization forward. Upper management and managers of the various functional units typically put together a set of policies that directly impact the employees, who, in turn, perform the daily work duties of the company.

This formula, however simple, is rarely performed with precision or effectiveness. The procedures and action steps to do work effectively are usually not written down. In many instances, work is done very informally without much attention paid to process. The end result of this is a disconnected company. Each individual carries on according to their own method, producing several different ways to perform the same function. With the repetition of this self-dictated process, a habit pattern is developed that becomes a "comfort zone." The problem with this method is that no one takes the time to determine the best way to perform any given function. Instead, people continue on separate paths even though their approach may be ineffective. A chain reaction is then set in place when the desired results are not achieved. Managers get upset and typically use punitive measures with an individual who thought he was simply doing his work. The fallout from this is lower morale and lack of productivity. At the end of the domino effect are the employees, who lose the commitment necessary to raise their level of performance.

Instead of the "every man for himself" approach, we all need to focus on continuous improvement. This includes not only the work produced but also the morale of the employees. If we focus on moving forward in a positive way for everyone, progress will follow. So, let's take some time to define the key criteria we're talking about.

1. Productivity: effective utilization of resources to achieve quality results within a specified time frame.

   a. Resources include people, tools, equipment, material, money, information, training, procedures, support, etc.

    b. Set a reasonable target date to complete the project, taking into account the complexity of the task at hand and the skills of the employee.

2. <u>Process</u>: a series of written activities or steps that need to be followed in order to achieve desired results.

3. <u>Procedure</u>: a "how to" course of action to get something done accurately.

4. <u>Standard</u>: a measurement that represents desired performance.

5. <u>Commitment</u>: a promise to carry out all assigned job responsibilities in an effective and efficient manner.

Without the proper attention to these key criteria, a sense of confusion filters down to the lower levels of the organization about what is expected of them. Employees are unsure of the correct process so they simply do the best they know how. This usually occurs because of a lack of connection from the top down. Management is detached from the needs of the supervisors and employees who have to do the work. The traditional management style of telling people what to do and how to do it is archaic. Without employee "buy-in" and involvement in the process, the results are lack of productivity and inefficiency. The need for change is clear, and the extent to which productivity improves has much to do with management's willingness to abandon the traditional approach of managing from the top down.

The alternative is to build a team organization in which management and employees are committed to the Mission, Vision, and Values of the organization. In the team format, people understand how their own efforts fit into the objectives of their area of responsibility and the goals of the company.

Workers and managers establish cooperative, congruent goals and Action Plans for achieving them, so that they can be successful together. They explore and delve into problems by exchanging information, discussing opposing views openly, and creating solutions to eliminate them.

Teamwork becomes the company's approach to getting things done. The company as a whole envisions, unites, empowers, explores, and reflects. Teams believe that they share a common vision with other sectors and individuals. They have cooperative goals, complement each other, discuss problems, recommend solutions, and strengthen their work relationships.

By creating a Team Organization, the following should occur:

1. An excitement about doing meaningful work.

2. An opportunity for people to speak their mind without repercussions.

3. Respecting and appreciating each other as people and contributors.

4. Confronting complex internal problems and blockages in a cooperative and positive manner.

5. Exploring problems by exchanging information and discussing opposing views openly and candidly with the intent to do what is best for everybody.

Building teamwork requires establishing some new traditions and making sure that all team players understand them while making a commitment to follow them. These "new traditions" are summed up as follows:

1. The Customer is the "Designated Driver."

    a. The organizations that change successfully are customer driven instead of   internally driven. This allows them to quickly and continuously understand, meet, and exceed their customer's changing expectations.

    b. Typically, the customer's list now expands to "better, faster, cheaper".

2. Let's Bridge the Gaps.

   a. A "stuck" organization is too functionally focused—a collection of separate functions that don't help each other.

   b. Overall, the common effect of a functional focus is to reduce quality while increasing the schedule and costs.

   c. A changing company must become process-focused. They need to consistently ask, "What is the best way to achieve desired results where everybody wins?"

3. Lead, Follow, or Get Out Of The Way.

   a. Most "stuck" organizations are management-centered. Managers see themselves as the central players in the organization and assume that they need to control everything.

   b. Employee involvement and teams must become the alternative because it is a better way to utilize all of the knowledge and skills of the entire organization.

Teamwork becomes the Management System that revolves around a process for improving productivity at all levels of the organization. The process is based on the concept of continuous improvement, which essentially means—"No matter where you're at you're never there." This gives the company a sense of motivation to strive for something better. It's not a quick fix, but a process where both management and employees are involved in facilitating change through effective leadership. In turn, the middle management team becomes the "glue" that ties together the three keys to collective success: direction from the top, support from the middle, and action by the employees at the bottom.

The Productivity Improvement Process is a collaborative course of action organized around four power points: Focus, Climate, Alignment, and Deployment. It includes the key ingredients that mix together as a recipe of winning ideas, strategies, and techniques

Leaders who are making the transition to this collaborative approach must buy into the Four Key Principles of Change.

1. Change takes time and requires patience and perseverance.

2. Change is a process, not a "hodge-podge" of individual activities.

3. Change requires the persistence to stay on course while overcoming obstacles until everybody gets comfortable with the new way of doing things.

4. Change requires ongoing support as people stumble in their efforts to execute a new formula for day-to-day activities.

So, let us now move onward to productivity improvement. Let us make a promise to develop and practice the necessary skills that bring the Productivity Improvement Process to life. The key to success is to "Keep doing it until we get it right." There are no short cuts. Follow the process, be patient, and everyone will reap the benefits of continuous improvement in action.

Why Teamwork?

Teamwork is defined as a cooperative effort between people in which individual interests are set aside for achievement of the common goal. It combines expertise to explore problems and conflicts and to develop solutions for everyone's mutual benefit.

A team is a group of high energy people who are individually different with diverse skills who blend together to achieve a common goal.

The question may arise: "Why teamwork?" By implementing the team concept, the following benefits accrue for the organization:

1. By using a collection of team member talents, quality decisions are the result.

2. By involving people from different functions to solve problems, we are combining ideas to come up with the best solution.

3. Involving people in decision-making increases employee morale and job satisfaction.

4. Synergy is created through the combined effort of team members which produces results greater than individual effort.

What do leaders have to do to develop a team organization? They need to do the following to make teamwork a reality:

1. Envision: They have to be visionaries—rise above the status quo and look for better and more productive ways to achieve desired results.

2. Unite: They convince people how working together spurs innovation, improves productivity, and makes people feel like important contributors to the success of the organization. By being united, people are able to express their individuality.

3. Empower: Leaders demonstrate to people that through teamwork, risks are encouraged, new processes are developed, and practical

procedures are put in place. They give people the "green light" for innovation and experimentation so that the collective ideas can be tested before being set aside.

4. Explore: Collaboration becomes the strategy for solving problems and looking for better ways to do things. Opposing views are discussed openly and directly so that practical, useful solutions can be developed and implemented.

5. Reflect: How can we improve? Are we as effective as we could be? Organizations don't want to get "stuck-in-the-mud." Accepting the status—quo is not the correct policy. Reflection requires measuring how well we're doing. When the organization is not getting better, it's time for the team to explore better ways of achieving desired results.

If managers and supervisors want to build teamwork, they must understand that the process of change requires patience. It becomes necessary to move away from a culture where managers think they have all the answers, make all the decisions, and tell people what to do. They begin to understand that building a team organization requires developing genuine relationships in a give-and-take atmosphere.

We must also keep in mind that leaders are at the center of creating a team organization. They must be empowered to challenge the status-quo while overhauling obsolete practices. Then a leader can empower others to make a difference. Issues must be explored thoroughly through the encouragement of diverse opinions. Opposing views can then be assembled into workable solutions. To make this happen, leaders must use the following strategies:

1. Bring together people with diverse backgrounds, expertise, outlooks, and functional experience—these people are likely to disagree.

2. Establish a basic rule: all ideas and views are encouraged, not rejected. There will be no repercussions for negative feedback.

3. Listening must occur. Everyone should pay attention and listen attentively to what each person is saying—acquire understanding through effective questioning.

4. Collect pertinent information by probing for underlying causes to problems.

5. Investigate when confusion arises about an issue.

6. Show respect to all individuals on the team. Critique ideas, not the person.

7. Consider and review all ideas. Use as many thoughts that contribute to the common goal or create a totally useful solution.

If we want to strengthen the organization through continuous improvement, the team approach is the way to go. Teamwork is successful because people want and need to be a part of something larger than themselves. People also feel the need to be respected by others. Teamwork provides the personal connection to others that we seek and allows us to feel accepted as key members of the team. Only then can we face the challenge of growth and accomplish extraordinary things with ordinary people.

It All Starts with Planning

Managing the job site is a team activity. To use a sports metaphor, the job site is like a football field. You can have the best quarterback of all time leading the way but if the wide receivers can't catch the ball, the team is going nowhere. It's much the same with the PM, Supt. and their "teammates".

Experience and skill as a PM and as a Supt. is clearly important but it is not the entire answer to success. To complete a major project, there needs to be a team of managers and workers in place who know what their roles are and how to accomplish the task at hand. In this regard, it is essential that the foreman knows who to turn to for assistance.

The first step is to form a planning team consisting of a Foreman, Superintendent, Project Manager (PM) and any other staff people who are relevant to the project.

The PM should lead the team through a review of the project, identifying objectives to be accomplished during each major phase of the work. A major key here is to listen carefully to everyone's ideas while encouraging further participation. If you have selected your team well, then the solutions should be right in front of you. So, simply listen to those solutions. If this meeting is conducted properly, you can save time and energy that will only lead to more profits down the road.

As your team develops a game plan, be sure someone accurately records it. Remember to distribute the meeting minutes to all members before the next meeting. Spend a little time at each session reviewing ideas from the last meeting; keep the good and discard the points that no longer make sense.

When the team feels good about the project plan, hold a major review process about all that has been decided—a dress rehearsal, if you will, of the building of the project. Keep an eye out for omissions or weaknesses that can impede progress in the operation. This process of streamlining will keep everyone on task with what is truly essential to moving forward. Distribute the plan to everyone who will be involved. Then, as the work advances, make everyone adhere to the plan. The key here is follow-up.

All in all, the planning sessions should resolve some key issues about the project:

- You should have identified the job-site staff, the General Supt., other Supt's, Project Engineers, Support Staff, etc.

- You should have assigned major project responsibilities. Remember, responsibilities are not always defined by titles or job descriptions.

- You should have identified all long lead time materials and services and arranged for timely procurement. Sort materials if necessary and make sure they get to the job site when needed.

- You should have created your progress schedule, if not in ultimate detail, at least in general form.

- One important item often overlooked in the planning stages is the flow of men, materials and equipment around the jobsite. A few minutes lost each day can greatly impair a tight schedule, especially if the time is lost by not maintaining a steady work flow.

- You should have planned for safety. Preliminary planning should recognize potential safety hazards. If your planning has been thorough, progress should occur without too many problems. However, be attentive to warning signs so you can make adjustments as necessary.

A major part of any planning session is spotting these warning signs. It's always better to take care of problems sooner rather than later. Stopping in mid-operation to take care of a problem only leads to wasted time and money. With this in mind, here are some common warning signs to be aware of:

- Poor or negative attitudes of jobsite personnel can indicate confusion with or misunderstanding of the project game plan.

- A faltering project start may mean there has been poor communication of the game plan to jobsite personnel, suppliers or subcontractors. If this is the case, review the plan with them and get their input.

- A failure to meet scheduled activity completion dates may mean those responsible for the plan's execution aren't following up. There is no substitute for constant and intense attention to detail. Review submittal logs, clarification requests and correspondence to see if information is flowing freely to all involved.

- Constant failure of jobsite staff to complete work activities at or near predicted unit costs can mean your budget numbers were wrong or there were labor inefficiencies.

Although no plan is perfect, it certainly makes sense to use the team approach in preparing your jobsite plan. Input from varied parties will give you a better chance to cover all your bases. The diverse talents of the team members put you in a better position to increase productivity and profitability on each and every project. Remember, the whole is greater than the sum of its parts.

Planning & Coordinating the Job

Let us now delve deeper into the specifics about planning and coordinating the job. We know the "Why?" and the "Who?" of team planning—let's move on to the "What?" What follows is a detailed outline on the purpose and execution of planning.

I. Purpose and Content

To discuss and practice job planning and coordinating so that these principles can be effectively applied to on the job situations.

II. Introduction

    A. What is planning?

        1. Work we do to predetermine a course of action before the fact.

        2. Systematic approach to a job—it is logical.

        3. Enables you to determine what should be done, why, when, where, how and who.

    B. Why plan? What are the advantages?

        1. Prevents us from following our tendency to act before we think.

        2. Simplifies task and eliminates unnecessary work.

        3. Makes coordinated effort possible.

        4. Avoids costly mistakes.

        5. Allows most effective and efficient use of time, manpower, materials and equipment (time is money).

        6. Prevails all the time in your day-to-day thinking.

        7. Enables you to determine if you did what should have been done.

III. Essentials of Planning

    A. What is to be done?

        1. Describe the job—be specific and review the Scope of Work.

        2. Sequence the action steps. Prioritize by order of importance.

        3. Be sure everyone understands their role (make certain everyone is working toward a common goal—avoid misunderstandings).

B. Why did we prioritize the action steps the way we did?

  1. Give a specific reason. Provide justification for each step—makes us take a hard look at need. Protects against doing unnecessary work.

C. When is it to be done?

  1. When do we start? Expected time for completion as well.

  2. Establishes priorities (relative to other tasks).

  3. Allows us to determine number of people used, amount of work to be done, etc.

  4. Helps schedule materials, tools and equipment.

  5. Anticipate delays and changing priorities.

D. Where is it to be done?

  1. Be specific on location

  2. Anticipate special conditions or safety hazards.

  3. Locate materials and equipment properly.

E. How is to be done?

  1. Break down the job into a step-by-step procedure. Follow the process.

  2. Determine requirements for men, material, tools and equipment.

  3. Review work and safety practices.

  4. Are other departments involved? What approvals are needed?

  5. How will you coordinate with the other trades on the job?

F. Who is to do it?

  1. Determine number of people needed for the job.

  2. Involve them in all planning sessions.

G. Follow-up

1. Why is this necessary? We need to find out if work is progressing according to plan. Remember that no plan is perfect. Follow-up helps us adjust to emergencies, unexpected circumstances or changes in the schedule.

2. Who will do the follow-up?

Critical Factor #4

Meeting the Leadership Challenge

- Definition and Key Components
- Developing Leadership Effectiveness
- Leadership Mind Set
- Five Key Elements of Effective Leadership

Leadership
Definition & Key Components

Leadership is the ability to guide, direct and influence people. A true leader establishes a positive work climate and gains the cooperation of others through teamwork and effective relationships. Successful leaders understand that there are seven key values that affect worker productivity. They are as follows:

- Respect/Dignity
- Job with Meaning
- Bigger Picture Focus
- Involvement in Decision-Making
- Fairness
- A Place to Grow
- Return on Investment

The leader delivers these values by performing the following actions:

- Provide positive feedback to people when they do good work.
- Let people know how important they are for achieving success on the job. The effective leader believes that people are his most important asset.
- Treat people fairly by measuring performance against standards.
- Ask people for their input and ideas before making a decision.
- Provide ongoing training and coaching so that people can grow in their job.
- Provide some form of incentives for peak performance.

Many times, leadership is referred to as "people skills"—specifically, how a person behaves when interacting with others. It's also an adaptive skill because the effective leader knows that situations change all the time and differences develop between people. To get the most out of people, a leader needs to be flexible instead of rigid while adapting to changing situations as they arise. Finally, a leader knows how to communicate and deal with different personality types.

Developing Leadership Effectiveness

Everybody agrees that leading people is extremely important in the workplace. Since many people are not self-starters, we have to find ways to move people in a positive direction to achieve desired results. The best approach is to lead by example, which includes the following activities.

Project a winning attitude. Whether you are the Owner, Vice President, Project Manager, Superintendent, Foreman or Crew Leader, you must approach your job with an engaging outlook that projects success to those around you. When things go wrong, you need to be solutions-oriented. By responding positively to negative situations, you will enhance your credibility as an action-oriented manager who is willing to get involved when problems occur. Instead of yelling at people and blaming them for mistakes, work with them to identify the problem and resolve it.

Watch your style. What is your leadership style? To be effective, your style must include the following actions:

- Collaborate—work with your people to discuss solutions and obstacles.

- Be accessible. When somebody really needs your input on something, be there for them without griping or complaining.

- Provide positive reinforcement when people produce quality work or do more than what's expected. Be supportive rather than critical. Most importantly, be specific. Know exactly why you're giving positive feedback or else it will ring hollow. Make sure that it is due to progress or success on a job-related activity. Remember, in order to give positive feedback you must be aware of what is happening on the jobsite. This way, you can give positive reinforcement in a timely manner, when it will mean the most. Don't forget to give feedback based on small gains or contributions as well as large one's. Since people operate at varying degrees of effectiveness, don't ignore those that are small improvements—they're still improvements. When people realize that you care about their efforts, they will continue to produce.

- Be an active listener. You can't use ideas until you actively listen to what people suggest. When people come to you with a problem, make sure you get them to specifically identify the problem and its underlying causes. Then ask them if they have a possible solution. If their solution makes sense, have them implement it. This shows that you're really listening.

- Avoid blaming or criticizing others when a mistake occurs. Remember to attack the problem, not the person. When a person makes a mistake, ask them if they realize what they've done. If they do know, ask them to explain what went wrong. Avoid pointing out the mistake first. Next, ask them how they would fix it. If they respond with the correct measures, all you have to do is agree and suggest they use that solution the next time. If they don't realize they've made a mistake or don't know how to fix it, you must provide your expertise in a positive, supportive manner. Do some coaching.

- Adopt an action-orientation. Encourage your people to take action and develop a sense of urgency about the work they do. In tandem with this, tell them to be innovative by trying new or better ways of operating on a day-to-day basis. When something works, make sure they tell you about it so that you can share it with the rest of the organization. It's a "Ready-Fire-Aim" Strategy that lets people experiment while learning from their mistakes. Aim those ideas that work. Share them with others in the organization.

In the end, to be an effective leader, you have to step up to the plate and make it happen yourself. People will follow your lead if you go about your job with a winning attitude and create a positive work climate.

Establishing a Leadership Mind Set

Every great leader has to start with basics. The foundation for any person in charge begins with the Leadership Mind Set. If we start with the proper outlook before we embark on a project, success is already within our reach. With this in mind, let's look at some guidelines that go into the Leadership Mind Set.

- I need my people more than they need me.
- People are our most important asset.
- Be open to change. If it's not broke, break it!
- Build on people's strengths. Don't focus on their weaknesses.
- Bring out the best in people. Satisfy their self-esteem needs.
- Know where you want to go (the goal) and decide what you have to do to get there (the Action Plan).
- Create a climate where people really want to do their best.
- Success is energy well-directed. Create a "Solution-Orientation." The key is to focus as much energy as possible in the direction you want to move.
- Institute a framework for continuous improvement:
  - Celebrate the small successes you achieve.
  - Know what you're doing.
  - Set specific objectives and make sure your people know what they are.
  - Point out the benefits for achieving the objectives.
  - Encourage ideas from people that will make things better. Let people participate in the solutions.
- Learn to ask effective questions. They create ownership.
  - What do you need from me to succeed on this project?
  - What have you accomplished so far that you are pleased with?

- Which of the activities you are doing will be easy for you to accomplish?

- What do you need to overcome the difficult tasks?

- What ideas do you have that will get us the results we want?

- Create a Customer Service attitude with your people.

  - Instilling a positive customer service attitude requires a positive employee ethic.

  - The level of service an employee brings to a customer is a reflection of how well that employee feels served or how well his/her needs are being met by the organization.

  - We can only serve the external customer effectively to the extent that we serve each other.

  - To the extent that your people feel supported encouraged, nurtured and served, they will serve their internal/external customers.

- Implement the following key leadership practices:

  - Be aware of the needs of your people.

  - Understand that it's your behavior that has an impact on your people.

  - Develop a team mentality.

  - Mobilize the discretionary effort of your people and empower them.

  - Be proactive instead of reactive.

  - Be a model of personal responsibility.

  - Put people first.

  - Have high expectations for results.

  - Encourage feedback, admit mistakes and ask for help.

Remember—Real leadership comes from the inside out. This requires several difficult shifts in our thinking, which are:

- Let go of your ego-driven need to have your own answers all the time.

- Let go of your need for strict control and trust your people.

- Drop your need to be right.

- Drop your protective barriers, learn to be open and vulnerable.

Five Key Elements for Effective Leadership

Let's put it very simply. There are five key elements of leadership that need to be emphasized if your staff and field supervisors are to be highly productive with high morale.

1. Let Employees Know What's Expected

The supervisor and employee should reach mutual agreement in five basic areas:

- The work that an employee does or the major activities for which he or she is responsible.

- Where the job fits into the total picture and why it is important.

- The factors upon which performance will be evaluated including quality, quantity, job budgets, safety and material and equipment control.

- How and when performance will be measured. It may be through quantitative measures or a series of statements describing the conditions which will exist when that area of the job has been adequately performed.

- How performance will be rewarded, e.g., a pay for performance system.

2. Let Employees Know Where They Stand

This means to accentuate the positive. Give your employees positive reinforcement when they do something well. Recognition cannot amount to a superficial pat on the back and it is the results accomplished that should receive the emphasis. This correct type of recognition, like other leadership techniques, is another way of fostering mental and emotional involvement in a job. A strong sense of personal identification with organizational goals takes place because it is directly related to benefits for the individual. In this case, psychological reward is the form of recognition.

3. Establish a Sound Communications Network

Effective leadership requires a network of communication that is both company and employee centered. An approach to communication which goes beyond basic job information can accomplish several things. It promotes a sense of identification, a feeling of being a key member of the team. This in turn fosters the interest, commitment and closeness which are so important to harmony and cooperation. A sound communication system breeds involvement and decreases the likelihood of an employee stating, "I just do my job. That's what I'm paid for." When people feel like they're in on important matters, they're much more likely to work more effectively for the company.

4. Establish a Positive Work Climate

- Give people the freedom to do their work without constant interference.

- Take positive action to contribute to employee growth and development.

- Discuss possible causes of and solutions to specific problems which are making an employee's job difficult.

- Train and coach the employee to find better ways of doing the work.

- Provide help and assistance in problem-solving as opposed to always giving the answer.

- Seek out and use employee ideas on how to do the job rather than always projecting the classic "my way or the highway" image.

- Be totally approachable so as to build something beyond a formal boss/employee relationship.

5. Be an Effective Delegator

Every time a supervisor delegates work to an employee three actions are either expressed or implied:

- He/she assigns duties, indicating what work the employee must do.

- He/she grants authority. Along with permission to proceed with the assigned work, he/she will probably transfer to the employee certain rights, e.g., the right to spend money, to direct the work of other people, to purchase materials, to represent the company to customers or to take other steps necessary to fulfill the new duties.

- He/she creates an obligation. In accepting an assignment, a subordinate takes on an obligation to his boss to complete the job.

By recognizing that no delegation is complete without a clear understanding of duties, authority and obligation, a supervisor can often overcome a good deal of misunderstanding.

These attributes of delegation are like a three-legged stool. Each depends on the others to help support the whole and no two can stand alone.

Delegation means knowing how to handle and distribute responsibility, authority and accountability.

Implement the five basic key elements now, so you can begin your journey to becoming an effective leader.

Critical Factor #5

Organization & Alignment

- **Getting Organized**
- **Establishing a Results Approach**
- **Setting Production Goals and Monitoring Production**
- **Making Weekly Planning a Reality**
- **Closing Out the Job**

Getting Organized

Many contractors say that you must be organized to run smoothly. Organizing is the ability to systematically arrange all necessary pieces in the work process so that desired results can be achieved in a timely, efficient manner.

Organizing for the job requires:

- Dividing up work among crew members.
- Assigning work and providing clear instructions for implementing the assigned activities.
- Linking up the field with a support system.
- Define the Project Manager's role in supporting the job site Foreman.
- Planning and anticipating ongoing needs for job site productivity.

To effectively execute the skill of organizing the Foreman, Superintendent and PM, one must clearly understand what organizing entails. There needs to be a unity of purpose, which means all players in the construction process must understand the following key components:

1. The skill requirements for labor.

2. Expected results of each person on the job.

3. Level of authority and clearly defined reporting relationships.

4. Feedback system.

5. Support from office to the field and how this support will occur.

6. Access to other necessary information which includes:

    - Scope of work
    - Budgets

- Blueprints, specs
- Schedule
- Procedures/paperwork requirements
- Job site meetings
- Access to office support staff
- Proper materials and correct amount
- Job site working conditions
- Training of people if skill deficiencies exist

To complete the organizing process, it is essential that the following job controls be put in place to ensure that the job site work process flows smoothly from beginning to end.

1. Pre-Job Planning Meeting/Pre-Job Review

This is usually the responsibility of the Project Managers and the size of the project usually dictates the amount of planning required. When considering such a meeting, you should consider the following items:

- Issuing a policy statement
- Who will attend
- Using a Pre-Job Planning Checklist with key items for job success
- Preparing written minutes of items discussed and distributing them to appropriate personnel.

2. Post Job Review

The purpose of the post job review is to review how the job came out and to provide feedback to all key parties (Project Manager, General Superintendent, Foreman & Estimator). This information will be used to avoid problems on similar jobs in the future. It's a "lessons learned" exercise that helps in improving productivity on future projects.

3. Tool & Equipment Inventory/Maintenance

Many times, tools and equipment are sent to jobs without a process for inventory control. It's important to maintain an inventory control of tools and equipment and have an M&R program in place to repair defective tools and equipment. To accomplish this end, you should consider implementing these three controls:

- Tool & Equipment Inventory Checklist
- Job site tagging procedures for defective tools and equipment
- Procedure for moving materials from the warehouse to the field and from the field to the warehouse and from job to job.

4. Job Site Safety Program

Implementing and maintaining an effective job site safety program is a must. To ensure that safety becomes a way of life on the job site, the following controls need to be put in place:

- Safety Rules Checklist
- Job Site Inspection Checklist
- Weekly Tool Box Safety Talk
- Hazard Communication Program
- Job Site Safety Program that includes:

  - Job Site Safety Inspection Report
  - Company's safety policy and safety rules
  - Format for Tool Box Safety meetings
  - Accident Reporting Procedures.

5. Job Site Paperwork

The reason for requiring the Foreman to complete paperwork on the job site has a lot to do with tracking productivity for the overall project. The office needs information from the field to determine the profitability of the job as it progresses. If the Foreman fails to maintain and report job site data to his Project Manager, then the company is really in the dark when it comes to determining how they did on a specific project.

An effective Job Site Reporting System should include:

1. A Daily Log

2. Weekly Job Progress Report

3. Daily Job Site Report

4. Expense Report for job site material purchases

5. Field Work Order for handling extra work requests.

6. Labor Tracking Process with key labor codes broken out by specific areas on job site.

Start using these Key Job Controls to improve overall productivity on the job site. Getting organized isn't easy, but it's a necessary skill for achieving desired results.

Establishing a "Results" Approach

The Foreman must communicate to his crew the results that are expected and then establish an Action Plan for achieving those results.

Expected Results

The Foreman needs to survey the job site and put the following pieces in place:

Productivity. Know the quality of work to be done in a specified time frame. Set production goals with your crew. "Do it right the first time according to the quality specs is essential. Review the customer's expectations with your crew.

Safety. Aim for an "accident free" job site. Implement safe work practices. Watch out for unsafe work conditions. Make sure everyone has the proper safety equipment and personal protective equipment. Enforce the safety rules.

Housekeeping. Eliminate clutter. Make sure your crew puts away all tools and equipment. Have your crew clean up their areas before going home.

Effective utilization of manpower, tools, equipment and material. Train your crew to utilize their tools effectively and to operate equipment properly and safely. Make sure they know what it takes to install material correctly. Tag all defective equipment.

Leadership. Maintain a positive work climate and build morale by utilizing the following key practices:

- Involve people in decision-making. Ask for their input and solve problems together.
- Treat people with respect.

- Provide positive feedback when people do good work and encourage feedback.

- Be visible and accessible.

- Support your people when they face adversity. Provide coaching when people have difficulty meeting standards.

- Communicate consequences for continued poor performance. Hold people accountable.

- Look ahead, plan and forecast future activities and the resources you'll need to accomplish desired results.

Developing the Action Plan ~ The Seven-Step Planning Process

1. Weekly Planning. Prepare a task list. What tasks do you have to do next week?

2. What are your material requirements? Know the quantity and type of materials needed and when they are needed (delivery date and time). Also, think about storage, location, protection and security.

3. What are your equipment requirements? What type do you need and how many of each type? When is the equipment needed? How long do you need it for? Make sure your crew knows how to safely operate this equipment.

4. Labor budget. Man-hours for each task; coding, tracking, feedback.

5. Crew size and needs. What skills do you want people to have (and be specific)? How many people do you need and when do you need them? Set production goals and collaborate with your crew.

6. Assigning work. Identify strengths. Assign work that people can do. Tell them to ask for help if they don't know how to do something. Provide feedback as to how they're doing.

7. Crew commitment. Get them to buy into the Game Plan for the job. Have your crew keep track of actual production and have them report

it to you. Listen to the crew members. They may have ideas on how to be more effective/efficient. Provide feedback on their progress.

Setting Production Goals and Monitoring Production

Setting Production Goals

A relatively small job of short duration does not require a complicated production schedule. On a one or two-man job, it should be relatively easy for the Foreman to communicate what he expects from his mechanics and then follow up to see that the work is done on time in a quality way.

On large jobs, the main consideration is that the Foreman gives his crew proper information and sets a realistic production goal with them. The Foreman must communicate the importance of production goals in achieving the overall schedule for the job. He must let his crew know that by achieving goals, they become key players in the construction process. The goals help create personal ownership for each crew member's contribution to the success of the job.

Once the goals are set, the Foreman must follow up and check on how the crew is progressing. If the crew member is on target, provide positive reinforcement. If he is not making progress toward the goal, then he must intervene and find out why. Then it is the Foreman's job to provide coaching to eliminate any barriers preventing the crew member from reaching the goal. The Foreman should be honest with his people. He should let them know where they stand. If they cannot reach their goal after repeated coaching, then he must let the crew member know that he cannot keep him on the job if improvement does not occur.

Tracking & Managing Labor

Your company should implement some form of production reporting by activity. Typically, these reports identify the amount of work that has to be done by activity, the estimated production and a place to record actual production.

It is the Foreman's responsibility to monitor the production by cost codes on a daily basis and record actual production. If the Foreman determines he is having difficulty meeting the specified productions, he should contact his superintendent and ask for help identifying the problem and establishing a game plan to get back on track.

Paying Attention to Ongoing Activities

As the job progresses, there are key activities that the Foreman must pay attention to in order to achieve optimum productivity on the job site. Since the basic resources of manpower, material, equipment and time must be provided to the Foreman as the job progresses, it is important for the Foreman to carry out the following responsibilities:

Scheduling and Crew Size—It's important for the Foreman to determine his average crew size. He should review his production report to get the total man-day count for each task and then look at the general contractor's schedule that shows the total number of working days for each function.

For example, let's say there are 20 man-days budgeted for a specific activity and the General Contractor's schedule shows a total of ten working days to perform the task. The size of your crew is determined as follows:

$$\frac{\underline{20 \text{ man days}}}{10 \text{ work days}} = \qquad 2 \text{ man crew for 10 days}$$

Knowing this, the Foreman should then do the following:

- Review the schedule with other subcontractors' Foremen. Find out if they will complete their work in time for your crew to come in and get their work done.

- Meet with the General Contractor's superintendent prior to mobilization in a particular area to address any obstacles that could interfere with the schedule and figure out what adjustments could be made to accommodate the needs of both parties.

- Review daily production results to determine if your crew is meeting their production goals, do some investigating to find out why and establish a game plan to eliminate the obstacles. If you're not sure of what to do, ask your superintendent for help. Remember, it's the Foreman's job to adjust his crew size up or down to make sure the work gets done on schedule.

Materials Management—Ordering

After discussing material needs at the Pre-Job Planning Meeting, the Foreman should meet with his Project Manager and Superintendent to determine long lead time items as well as special sizes that may be needed for special materials. Review submittals after they've returned and make any adjustment to the material list.

Some other things to do are as follows:

- Discuss with the crew any requirements they might have.

- Plan and order equipment and materials a week in advance.

- Coordinate deliveries to reduce the number of trips to your job site.

- Order material in the following sequence—

  - Communicate the job name and number, the type and amount of materials needed and delivery dates.

  - Identify and communicate where you want the materials dropped off on the job site and specify any special equipment you may need to unload the material.

Receiving Materials

- Plan and clear out an area where the materials will be located and stored.

- Upon delivery, make sure you have received the right amount, type and condition of materials. Upon verification of proper quantities, type, sizes and condition, physically count the pieces to ensure that you got what you ordered. Then sign and date the receiving ticket.

If there is a discrepancy, indicate such on the receiving ticket and notify the Project Manager about the discrepancy.

Tools, Equipment and Scaffolding

- The Foreman should plan his equipment and tool needs weekly and communicate those needs to the warehouse one week in advance.

- He should monitor and check how people are using the equipment on a daily basis. He should make sure his crew knows how to operate the equipment safely and how to maintain it after using it.

- Tag all defective equipment and specify on the tag what the defect is.

- Return all equipment and tools that are not currently needed on your project. Be sure you understand the procedure and paperwork required for ordering, transferring and returning tools and equipment.

- Maintain an inventory of tools and equipment on a weekly basis.

Making Weekly Planning a Reality

The timing and quality of planning is a significant factor in determining the success of any project. Job supervision and project management begin with planning. The performance of even the most effective supervisor can be undermined by ineffective or incomplete planning. You must control the work rather than letting the work control you. You can achieve control by adequately planning each work element.

A plan is a "road map" to get from one place to another. This is what you must do:

1. Set a production goal. Remember, you have four primary responsibilities.

    •   Complete the assigned work within the budget.

    •   Complete the assigned work on time.

    •   Complete the work in a safe manner.

    •   Deliver quality workmanship.

2. Determine what must be done to achieve you goal.

    •   Have a game plan—know work requirements for which your crew is responsible.

3. Determine how to do it.

    •   Identify resources (material, equipment, labor and procedures) you need to do the task properly.

Develop a Weekly Planning Sheet that the Foremen have to complete on a weekly basis. It's important for Foremen to develop the habit of writing things down and by doing so, they will realize three important benefits:

1. They can focus their attention on the job and its requirements instead of concentrating on remembering details.

2. They will have a ready checklist to consult anytime; They will not for-
    get—no matter how much pressure they are under.

3. They will free their mind for creative thinking about their daily plans,
    job requirements, and the situations at hand.

The Weekly Planning Sheet should include the following information:

- A "Description of Work" column for listing trade specific work by
  area. For each day of the week, specify the number of tradesmen
  that will be working on each activity listed.

- Another column should be titled "Estimated Work Completion
  Date" and the Foreman will estimate the completion date for each
  work activity.

- The Foreman will note in another column entitled "Note Manpower #of Layoffs or Add." This is the number of tradesmen he will
  need to layoff or add for each work activity. If he's forecasting layoffs or additions, he should communicate this information to his
  Supt. right away.

- The Foreman should forecast the required tools/equipment/materi-
  als needed to complete the next week's listed work activities. Get
  this information to your Warehouse Coordinator right away. If the
  tools/equipment/materials are required from suppliers, notify your
  Project Manager right away.

- If sub-contractors are being used on the job, the Foreman will
  schedule the next week's work activities for subs under another column entitled, "Sub-contractors."

- The Foreman should plan alternative work possibilities in case the
  "planned for" work activities are not available. This information
  should be provided under a column entitled, "Alternate Work
  Schedule."

- The Foreman should send the Weekly Planning Sheet to the office
  with all other required paperwork by designated deadline. A copy
  should go to the Supt. for his review and follow-up.

Also, when the Foreman gets involved in the planning activity, he should ask himself the following questions and make sure he gets answers to these questions:

1. Do I have a clear understanding of the scope of work?

2. What is the time frame and budget for each phase of the job?

3. What job conditions am I faced with?

4. How will I coordinate activities with the other subs?

5. What are the critical standards of performance?

6. What is the plan for checking ongoing progress on the project?

7. When will the Pre-Job Planning Meeting be scheduled?

Remember, it's the Foreman's job to be productive on the job site. But, without the ability to plan effectively, he is unlikely to be successful. If the Foreman doesn't plan, he will be ineffective and the job will end up controlling him. Chaos and disorganization will be the result. This can be avoided through effective weekly planning—JUST DO IT!

Closing Out The Job

The Foreman, Project Manager, and Superintendent all play a part in carrying out the following key job close out activities:

1. Punch List

As the project winds down, the Foreman should develop a plan for removing the equipment, tools, and excess material from the job site.

The Foreman also needs to develop a Punch List while the job is still mobilized, and he should coordinate this Punch List preparation with the Superintendent and the Project Manager. The Foreman could also invite the G.C.'s Superintendent to walk the job together to develop the Punch List. If this is not an option, the Foreman should develop the Punch List and then review it with the G.C's Superintendent.

The G.C.'s Superintendent may have items to include on the Punch List, or he will have prepared his own Punch List. Compare your list with his and agree on a final Punch List. He should also give a copy to the Project Manager and his Superintendent.

The Punch List items should be completed in one week, or within a time frame agreed upon with the G.C.'s Superintendent. Have the G.C.'s Superintendent sign off on the completed Punch List to verify that all items were completed. Send a copy of the completed Punch List to the Project Manager.

2. Notification of Job Completion

When the job is completed, the Foreman should notify his Superintendent, who, in turn, will notify the Project Manager so that he can finalize the contract amount; clearly document a list of extras on the job, and complete the necessary paperwork so that appropriate parties can be notified to carry out specific responsibilities which are as follows:

- Warehouse Manager/Coordinator provides notification when to pick up the material and equipment on the job site.

- Superintendent provides information about availability of manpower for future jobs.

- Construction Manager notifies Accounting that the job is completed and that there will not be any more labor costs to be charged to the job.

- The Construction Manager and owner have final approval for contract amount and verifies that all material and other costs have been charged to the job.

- Accounting ensures that final billing can be generated and we can collect our money before our lien rights run out.

3. Customer Post Job Review

When the job is completed, the Project Managers should conduct a Post Job Review with the customer (their Project Manager and Superintendent).

This is an opportunity to get feedback about the "positive's" and "needs improvement" areas. The things that were done well should be shared with other Foremen. You want to find out where you need to improve so that you can ensure the G.C. that all problems reported will not be repeated on future jobs. Here are some questions for the customer:

1. Were the contract and submittals executed and returned in a timely fashion?

2. How did our Foreman interact with the G.C.'s Superintendent?

3. How did we: (Foreman; Supt.; PM).

   - Expedite changes?

   - Help solve problems?

   - Help coordinate with other trades?

- Maintain the project schedule?
- Do in terms of quality workmanship?

4. How was our safety performance?

5. How would you assess our housekeeping on the job?

6. How would you rate our crew's daily production?

7. What specific areas do you feel we need to improve on?

8. Would you want us back on future jobs?

4. Internal Post Job Review [Lessons Learned]

The Project Manager should schedule and conduct an internal Post Job Review when the job is finished. The Project Manager should invite the following people to attend:

Construction Manager	Foreman
Superintendent	Safety Manager
Warehouse Coordinator	Estimator/Salesman

The Project Manager will use a Post Job Review Checklist to conduct the meeting.

5. Demobilize Effectively

The Foreman should conduct a Final Job Walk Around to ensure that all of the equipment is ready to be returned to the Shop or Warehouse. A final inventory of tools, equipment, and materials should be taken and reviewed with the Superintendent. They will determine what will be returned to the Warehouse and what items will be disposed of on the job site.

The final inventory should be compared to the initial tool and equipment inventory with an explanation about missing items. It's important that accountability exists for tools and equipment so that sound cost controls can be maintained for all jobs.

Also, make sure the Project Manager conducts the following activities to effectively close out the job:

- Finalize contract amount with customer completely so that a final billing can be submitted and the money owed can be collected before the Lien Rights run out.

- Pursue any and all change orders diligently with the G.C.

- Get prepared for any back charge negotiations.

Remember, closing out the job is a critical activity that must be carried out effectively so that you can maximize productivity on future jobs.

Critical Factor #6

Motivation

- **Developing Motivation Power**
- **Establishing a Motivational Climate**

Developing Motivation Power
~ The Six Keys ~

It is a Foreman's responsibility to establish a positive work climate so that his crew wants to come to work and do their best work every day. But it's important to remember that the Foreman really only has power over the climate, not over the people. The climate of the workplace needs to emphasize trust, commitment and achievement of key results. Everyone on the crew must be on the road to continuous improvement by being more cost-conscious, empowered, self-directed, high performing, ethical, urgent, balanced, customer and team focused. To achieve this tall order of necessities, the Foreman must motivate his crew by doing the following:

1. Gaining Commitment

The Foreman must explain to his crew what their role is in achieving optimum productivity on the job site. He must review the job schedule with them and explain the quality specifications. He must explain the importance of setting production goals with them so that they can meet the General Contractor's schedule. To create commitment requires that the Foreman and his crew promise to do whatever it takes to achieve the production goals every day. The Foreman must provide his crew with the necessary resources to achieve their goals and offer support and assistance when they need his help.

2. Encouraging Growth

The Foreman must stress to his crew how important it is for them to continually learn how to do things better and to improve their skills. He must provide ways for them to do that.

3. Creating Conviction

The Foreman has to get his crew believing that they can achieve their goals. This means that they have to leave their comfort zone and keep striving to do things better. He must get them to keep moving forward, especially when obstacles occur. He must take the leadership role and never go back to the old way of doing things.

4. Creating Connection

The Foreman must build teamwork by emphasizing to his crew how important it is for them to work together and help each other. It's the concept that "We're all in this together." The goal is to create synergy with the underlying idea being that the team is more powerful than the individual. He must encourage them to ask for help when they face situations they don't know how to handle. It takes a team of connected players to achieve success on the job.

5. Creating Ownership

It is the Foreman's responsibility to get his crew to take ownership for their job. He can accomplish this by clearly explaining what he expects from them. He should give his people the resources they need to be effective and provide coaching when his people need help. He should give people the freedom to do their job without interference and provide positive reinforcement when workers do well.

6. Building Relationships

If we want people to come to work and do their best work every day, then we must establish positive relationships with them and identify what they need to be effective in their jobs.

In order to accomplish all of this, we must understand what it takes to motivate people to become peak performers. This requires us to have a basic understanding of motivation and what we can do to make motivation a reality in the day-to-day work situation. Motivation is an internal impelling influence or need that creates positive action or change. Motivation requires an understanding of several basic principles:

- There are short-term and long-term motivators. Short-term motivators are external to the individual and need to be done on a repetitive basis (for example, listening, providing positive feedback, giving someone a raise or promotion). If provided sporadically, they don't last very long. Long-term or internal motivators are triggered by identifying one's internal driving forces or "hot buttons" and then setting up situations or conditions where those internal driving forces can be satisfied through action.

- People are motivated by doing the things they like to do and doing what they are good at. They are not necessarily motivated by the things we want them to do, because what we want them to do may be something they don't like doing or are not very good at doing—a weakness rather than a strength.

- We can set the stage for others to motivate themselves by understanding what makes them tick as well as giving them the opportunity to act out their internal driving forces.

- People have different behavioral styles and to establish positive relationships with them requires understanding why they act the way they do.

- We must understand that people want to be effective in their jobs. They want to do a good job. It is important to identify people's strengths and to set up conditions where those strengths can be applied in their work situation.

- We must accept the fact that people are different and different is normal. It is the blending of differences and allowing for people to do what they're good at that motivates them to function as key members of the team.

- Learning how to communicate with people who have different behavioral styles builds strong partnerships in an environment of teamwork.

Establishing a Motivational Climate

The Foreman not only has to identify what makes people tick, but also has to put a process in place that facilitates peak performance. When people can do the things they're good at, receive all of the resources they need to be effective and have processes to follow that lead to quality results and good morale, then peak performance can become a reality.

What follows is the recommended process for establishing a motivational climate that leads to peak performance.

Implementing a Feedback System

Feedback is necessary if the Foreman is to achieve open, honest, two-way communication between the job site and the office. Without this form of reciprocity, the company will simply get "stuck in the mud". Feedback lets the Foreman know if he's on the right track or not. The Foreman is responsible for giving feedback to his crew and for encouraging feedback from his crew. Without feedback, problems do not surface in a timely manner and progress is stymied. Effective feedback provides the following benefits:

- It helps in identifying obstacles and barriers to productivity.
- It lets people know how they are doing.
- It fills gaps in knowledge.
- It lets people know where to take corrective action.
- It alleviates fear of the unknown.
- It is a means for building positive relationships and teamwork.

Managing Conflict

Conflict between people occurs quite often on a job site. Conflict is not something we plan for—it just happens! The Foreman has to learn how to deal with it and get it resolved.

Simply put, conflict is unresolved controversy that occurs due to one or more of the following:

- People not getting what they want or need.
- Differences in perceptions about expectations.
- Lack of information.
- Confusion about role demands.
- Lack of involvement in decision-making.
- Lack of explanations for pending changes.
- Duplication of work.
- Ineffective delegation.

Tips for Dealing with Conflict

1. It's okay to disagree. Someone may have a better solution than you.

2. Focus on the issue or problem, not the person. We all make mistakes.

3. Approach the person in a positive way. If you become negative, conflict will persist.

4. Deal only with behaviors, not attitudes. For example: "When you've finished your assigned task, please don't walk around and bother other people. Come and see me and I'll give you another job to do."

5. Stick to specifics, not generalities. Avoid saying something like, "Your quality is poor." Be more specific and identify why it is poor.

6. Deal with one issue at a time. If you take on too much, you may end up treating symptoms rather than dealing with the underlying causes.

7. Identify what the other person wants. Then decide if you're willing to give that person what he/she wants. If not, what's your fallback position?

8. Mutually agree on action to be taken. Both of you have to participate in the solution.

9. Set up a follow-up date to review how things worked out.

Six Steps for Resolving Conflict

1. Define the real problem based on the information available to you. Investigate and identify the underlying causes.

2. Get together and identify what each of you want.

3. Approach each other in a positive way—avoid blaming or being accusatory. Communicate specifically, honestly and openly—but don't become personal.

4. Develop Action Plans to satisfy each other's wants.

5. Make a commitment to carry out your end of the bargain. Avoid making excuses.

6. Establish a follow-up date to measure results.

Negotiation

Negotiation is an interactive, cooperative process in which people attempt to resolve conflicting needs and demands. Those engaged in the negotiating process need to understand that it includes the following key elements:

- It is the art of compromise and accommodation.

- It is based on a "needs" focus.

- Its objective is to achieve mutual agreement.

- The parties involved must understand that they both may perceive the same situation differently.

- It is the most appropriate response to conflict situations. (Conflict is defined as any situation where people have differing interests and both parties could be affecting each other's pursuit of those interests).

Collaboration is the best approach to effective negotiation. Here are the requirements for effective collaboration.

1. Openness and Trust: Present your side of the story without blaming the other person. Also, state that you would like to do what's necessary to resolve the issue.

2. Empathy: Really work at understanding the other person's point of view without being judgmental.

3. Be Supportive: Do what you can to help the other person get what he/she wants.

4. Be Postive: Work toward identifying positive actions to resolve the problems.

5. Equality: Avoid using Position Power to resolve the issue. Treat each other as equals.

6. Emotional Control: Stay calm. Don't let your emotions take over. If you do, listening stops.

7. Listen Actively: Gain understanding as to where the person is coming from. Ask key questions and don't interrupt the other person while he/she is talking.

8. Be Creative: Both of you may have to come up with some new ideas to resolve the issue since there may be no available information to deal with the issue.

Five Steps for Negotiating Effectively

1. Separate the Person from the Problem
    You may want to clearly understand the other person's perception

since that's their reality. Avoid blaming the other person for the problem. Get to the underlying causes.

2. Focus on Interests, Not Positions
    For example, the GC's Supt. is interested in meeting the schedule for the job. So are you. However, your positions, or how you will meet the schedule, may be very different. Understand the other person's position and if you disagree with it, present your position and how it will satisfy the other person's interests.

3. Generate a Variety of Alternative Solutions
    Be creative. Each person should come up with ideas that could achieve desired results. The more ideas that are available from both sides will allow both parties to participate in the solution.

4. Base Agreement on Objective Standards and Fair Procedures
    The objective standard is getting the job done on time according to procedures that are ethical and legal. You may have to develop new procedures if none are available for dealing with the issue. There may be no precedent previously set for the situation being negotiated.

5. Have an Alternate Plan if Negotiation Fails
    This is called your Best Alternative to a Negotiated Agreement—your BATNA.

Critical Factor #7

The Customer

- Defining Customer Satisfaction
- Delivering Customer Satisfaction
- Moving Toward Customer Service Excellence
- Focusing on Great Performance for Customers

Defining Customer Satisfaction

How well are you serving your customers? This question pertains to both internal and external customers. The internal customers are those people inside the company in which you work with and interact. For example, the Foreman's internal customer is the Superintendent, the Project Manager, office staff personnel, i.e., Payroll Administrator and the crew. Everyone has one or more internal customers and the key for internal customers is to interact positively with them and satisfy their needs. The same would be true of external customers who are the G.C.'s Superintendent, the Architect, the Owner, and the other trades on the job.

A key concept of customer satisfaction is this: The level of service an employee brings to a customer is a reflection of how well that employee feels served, or how will his/her needs are being met by the organization. You can only serve the external customer satisfactorily to the extent that internal customers serve each other (developing an internal needs orientation). To the extent that internal customers feel supported, encouraged, nurtured and served, they will then help their external customers.

What is a *customer?*

C someone who has **concerns** and needs to be **communicated** with.
U someone who requires **understanding**.
S expects top-notch **service**.
T wants **tangible** results.
O wants an **organizational** commitment that his needs will be satisfied.
M **meet** his deadlines.
E expects high **energy** and **enthusiasm** from those with whom he does business.
R expects **reliability** and **responsiveness**.

To provide a high level of customer satisfaction, you must meet the following requirements:

1. Create W.O.W.
   "Work on Winning:" Establish Win/Win relationships—be action-oriented by giving the customer what he wants first, you'll probably get what you want. A genuine customer focus.

2. Act Like you're the Company
   No matter who you are or what you do, the behavior you transmit to the customer creates a perception that leads to an evaluation of the total company. If the Foreman is argumentative and surly with the G.C.'s Supt. and gets into the "blame game" with him, then the Supt. will generalize and tell the people in his company that your company is nothing but trouble and refuses to satisfy the needs of the G.C. This is a good way to get removed from the bid list.

3. Be Competent and Care.
   This requires people who know what their talking about and know how to solve problems, meet the schedule, and produce quality results. They're proactive rather than reactive. They also project a "Whole Job" focus and care about the G.C.'s problems and help solve them.

4. Honesty is the Only Policy.
   When there's a problem or an obstacle that prevents you from being effective and efficient, you present your case to the G.C. without emotion and offer a solution to solve the problems or remove the obstacle. Be candid without attacking the person but have the facts and display a willingness to help.

5. Listen—It creates trust and respect.
   Hear people out. Let them finish what they're saying. Don't interrupt them while they're talking—gain an understanding of the issue, problem, or need and let them know you're there to move forward and make things better.

6. Provide Exceptional Service.

    Impress your customers. Do more than what's expected. Go the "extra mile." Provide value, which is in the eyes of the beholder. Find out what's really important to your customer and then deliver it.

7. Be a Fantastic Fixer.

    There's a solution for every problem. Let the customer know that you will do whatever it takes to solve the problem. Even if you don't have the answer, you will go to other people in your company who have the knowledge and expertise to solve the customer's problems. Utilize Team Concept—you don't have all the answers so find and use those that do.

8. Master the Art of Calm.

    Always control your emotions. Yelling, screaming, and letting your emotions take over communicates immaturity and ends up with a lot of arguing and animosity. It creates problems instead of solving them. By controlling your emotions and expressing dissatisfaction in a straight-forward, assertive way opens the door to mutual respect and problem resolution.

Delivering Customer Satisfaction

This section defines what the Foreman can do to deliver a high level of customer satisfaction to the GC. The Foreman needs to adopt the principles of the R-A-T-E-R Concept and deliver that concept through day-to-day actions.

R-A-T-E-R Concept

R—Reliability

- Consistency of action. Perform within authorized boundaries.
- Meet the schedule and deliver the scope.
- Follow through and do what you say you will do.
- Be visible and accessible.
- Lead the crew and maintain work flow.
- Demonstrate personal accountability.
- Satisfy G.C.'s needs and expectations in a positive, effective manner.

A—Assurance

- Become the expert in your job.
- Understand and help the G.C.'s Supt. to meet his goals.
- Know the strengths of your crew.
- Display a "service attitude." Show you care about the total job.
- Be capable and confident in what you do.
- Meet the quality standard.
- Do everything you can to keep the work in sequence.
- Have a track record of achieving positive results.
- Ongoing planning and organizing.

T—Tangible Results

- Meet the schedule and time frames for each phase.
- Deliver quality work on time with sound safety practices in a positive work climate.
- Forecast needs—then plan for and deliver them.
- Keep striving for perfection.
- Only promise what you can deliver. Specify exactly how you will get there, then do it!

E—Empathy

- Clearly understand the G.C.'s position. Have a Big Picture Focus.
- Display concern for the G.C. Supt's problems. Help solve them.
- Keep ongoing contact with G.C.'s Supt. Let him know you are there to provide service.
- Speak up at weekly job site progress meetings. When you have suggested solutions to problems, be willing to execute the solution.
- Be respectful of the G.C.'s Supt.
- Understand before you react.

R—Responsiveness

- Respond to and resolve problems quickly—don't procrastinate. Do not put critical issues on the back burner.
- Display a sense of urgency.
- Adapt to changing situations.
- Get the G.C. out of a jam when you can.
- Always have a target date for getting something done. Start right away.

These are the keys to maximizing customer satisfaction. Before you implement these keys, take some time to answer the following questions, and then develop your Action Plan for delivering a high level of customer satisfaction.

1. What do your customers really want from you?

2. Do you have the necessary resources (expertise, people, equipment, ideas, information) to give your customers what they really want?

3. Customers buy value. Do you know what your customers value?

4. Do you know what quality is in the eyes of the customer?

5. What obstacles prevent you from delivering a high level of customer satisfaction?

Moving Toward Customer Service Excellence

"Restless Dissatisfaction with the Status Quo."

This is the definitive statement for customer service excellence. As always, it starts at the top of the organization with management adopting the following philosophy: "We can and will do better." Once adopted, it is a matter of designing the corporate value system and building those values into every aspect of the management/employee relationship. It continues with upper management's commitment to establishing and reinforcing new standards of service excellence in every facet of the company.

Managing an organization's human resources is inextricably linked with managing its customer relations. To enjoy the highest standards of service excellence, organizations must have motivated employees and managers. To have this is to have teamwork.

Teamwork promotes positive innovation in all human resource areas:

- Excitement about the company's vision.
- A strong desire to serve customers well.
- Ongoing communication that is focused on results.
- A continuous striving to make improvements on the job.
- Asking for assistance when necessary.
- The freedom to speak their minds.
- Everybody feels important, valuable and included; not just those in top positions.
- Forgiving slights, misunderstandings and opposition.

Action Teams are formed to serve as a coalition of people dedicated to solving complex internal problems and customer demands. Comprised of a diverse group, the Action Teams listen with an open mind to opposing positions, hammer out recommendations that make sense from a number of perspectives and they work to develop sound solutions that deserve their commitment.

Teamwork is the essential ingredient to satisfying the needs of both its internal and external customers. Teamwork provides everyone with the following:

- A shared commitment to service excellence.
- Understanding that their personal job security is totally dependent on their company's ability to impress customers and make them want to come back.
- Knowing that providing excellent service is in their best interests.

Building a team with this kind of commitment to customer service requires laying a foundation based on the premise that teamwork creates excellence in employee relations. When employees see themselves as important assets to the company's growth and success, they will then willingly practice the behaviors that bring about customer service excellence.

Focusing on Great Performance for Customers

Quality is whatever the customer says it is. We must actively reach out in order to identify and understand the needs and desires of our customers if we are going to delight and impress them with great performance. Thinking strategically begins with us, not with our customers. By asking the following questions, we will be able to identify what great performance is from the perspective of our customers.

Productivity

Once you've been awarded the job, review the following items with the GC to make sure you satisfy their requirements. Request that a pre-planning meeting be held to discuss these items?

- Scope of Work: What specifically do you want us to do?

- Budget: Quantity of work; man-hours or man-days to complete the job schedule.

- Quality specifications: Materials and workmanship requirements.

- Procedures: Do you want us to do the work in a certain way? What is the work plan?

- How much work do you expect us to get done each day? Each week?

- By what method can we review progress on the job? Weekly walk-arounds with a key person to monitor and assess how we're doing can allow for quick action to be taken to resolve problems.

- How often do you want to see the project manager or have communication with him?

Service

- How do you define excellent customer service? What is really important to you once we start the job?

- Where do you want us to locate our trailer?

- How long do we have to remove the material and equipment off the job-site when the job is finished?

- We'd like to locate the materials when they're delivered as close to our crew's working area as possible. Is it okay with you?

- When a problem occurs on a job, how do you want us to handle it? Is there someone you want us to contact when a problem occurs that requires your involvement?

- Can we communicate with you when we see additional work opportunities? To whom should we talk about such opportunities (T&M work)?

- What do you consider to be your biggest obstacles on the job and how can we help you eliminate them?

Safety

- Do our safety requirements coincide with yours? If not, where do we differ and what are the specifics of your safety requirements? May we have a copy of your safety rules?

- What working conditions will we be exposed to (heat, cold, tight space, etc.)? We need to identify people who can work under those conditions.

- What are your housekeeping requirements?

Paperwork/Changes

- What paperwork documentation requirements do you want us to follow? Do you have any special paperwork requirements?

- How do you want us to handle requests for changes or additional work? What about extras? What do you consider billable extras?

- Who has to approve additional work requests before billing taking place?

- What are your billing requirements?

Dependability

- What do you expect from the Foreman and his crew (hours of work, breaks, lunch, wash-up time, leaving at the end of day, washroom facilities)?
- Who do you want attending your job-site meetings?
- What qualities/skills do you expect a Foreman to have?

Security

- What are your job security requirements?
- What areas do we have access to? Which ones should we stay away from? Are there certain times of the day that we can work in certain areas?
- What entrance/exits can we use to deliver and remove equipment/materials from the job-site?

When you have the answers to these questions, you will be able to provide your customer with a great performance and provide your company with great referrals and future jobs.

Critical Factor #8

Developing People

- **Key Elements of Effective Supervision**
- **How to Retain Good Employees**

Key Elements of Effective Supervision

Successful contractors realize the importance of supervisory development because they realize the importance of improving employee productivity. By recognizing this necessity, they can increase their profits by controlling their labor costs so that they can more successfully bid on jobs and complete them at a lower cost than the job estimate.

A cost control program will not be effective unless it first focuses on improving productivity, and one of the essential ingredients of improving productivity is improving supervisory effectiveness.

Contractors need to display an organized image to people who come to work for them. When new employees join your company, they should be exposed to an orientation program that explains operating philosophy, policies and procedures, how employees will be evaluated, the pay system, and management expectations. All of these items should also be included in an Employee Handbook, which would be given to the employee at the orientation session.

Training of technical and supervisory skills must become a way of life in your organization. Your supervisors can provide technical training on the job by following these basic steps:

- Setting the atmosphere for training
- Training them thoroughly in their jobs
- Explaining and demonstrating the key technical skills
- Letting the employee do the job
- Following up to determine if the employee is doing the job properly

This technical training should be ongoing and continually reinforced. It can never stop.

You also have to expose your foremen and superintendents to management and leadership skills training. They need to be trained in the skill areas of:

- Planning, leading, organizing and controlling
- How to deal effectively with people
- Communication/Listening
- Motivating self and others
- Establishing a motivational climate
- Building teamwork
- Appraising performance
- Administering corrective discipline
- Managing Conflict
- Coaching Effectively
- Problem-Solving
- Negotiating

If your supervisors don't refine these skills, then increased productivity will not become a reality.

If contractors really want to improve productivity on the job site, they must continually develop their supervisors. It is through the supervisor that management objectives are achieved. Therefore, when choosing their supervisors, they must look for leadership. Supervisors must be proficient in the following skill areas if we expect them to lead effectively:

- They must first have a thorough knowledge and mastery of all the job skills and tools and equipment used by their crews.
- They must lead by example—by practicing good work habits they will gain respect and be more likely to instill these admirable qualities in their crews.

- They must be able to organize, anticipate and solve problems, make decisions, adjust to change, perform weekly planning and give comprehensible instructions to their crews before the job starts.

- They must show care and concern for their employees by helping workers improve when they make mistakes, rather than using criticism when mistakes are made.

- They need to make sure their crews have all the resources they need, encourage feedback, make suggestions, and give support.

How to Retain Good Employees

For any successful business, retention of good employees is a must. Good employees consistently work toward peak performance and can be counted on when obstacles arise.

The first guideline that needs to be established in order to retain good employees is that of a positive work climate. People who like coming to work tend to do their best work everyday. Establishing a positive work climate also makes people much more likely to become self-motivated and sustain their good work habits. With this in mind, employers need to get serious about following guidelines to retain good employees. Let's focus on six essential areas that will help in accomplishing this goal:

1. Providing ongoing training in technical, management and leadership skills. This type of training must become a way of life in your organization. Your supervisors can provide technical training on the job by following these basic steps:

   • Set the atmosphere for training.

   • Train the employees thoroughly in their jobs.

   • Explain and demonstrate the key technical skills.

   • Let the employee do the job.

   • Follow up to determine if the employee is doing the job properly.

   This technical training should be ongoing and continually reinforced. *It should never stop.*

   You also have to expose your foremen and superintendents to functional and adaptive skills training. They need to be trained in the following skills areas:

   • Planning, leading, organizing and controlling

   • How to deal effectively with people

   • Communication

- Motivating self and others
- Establishing a motivational climate
- Building teamwork
- Appraising performance
- Administering corrective discipline

If supervisors don't receive training in these areas, they may become disenchanted with the organization and then eventually leave (if you don't get rid of them first).

Supervisors must become proficient in the following leadership skills so that they can be effective in dealing with their people while achieving satisfaction from the work they do.

- They must first have a thorough knowledge and mastery of all the job skills and tools and equipment used by their crews.
- They must lead by example—by practicing good work habits they will gain respect and be more likely to instill these admirable qualities in their crews.
- They must be able to organize, anticipate and solve problems, make decisions, adjust to change, conduct pre-job planning sessions and give comprehensible instructions to their crews before the job starts.
- They must show care and concern for their employees by helping workers improve when they make mistakes, rather than using criticism when mistakes are made.
- They need to make sure their crews have all the resources they need, encourage feedback, make suggestions and give support.

2. Setting Goals
    Goal setting—which is setting specific, measurable targets to accomplish in a specified time frame—is extremely important because it is a tool for:

    - Monitoring worker performance—since workers need to know how they're performing.

- Giving workers direction, so that they know what's expected of them and, as a result, have a clear focus on what has to be done.

- Involving workers in the overall work plan by asking them for their input prior to setting goals that affect their team.

Through goal-setting employees feel like they're key members of the team. When employees feel that way, there's little chance that they will leave.

3. Providing Incentives
   Incentives are tangible rewards that are given to those who are peak performers and make positive contributions to the profitability of the company. You need to pay incentives for the critical factors affecting productivity, such as:

   a. Effective labor management and quality: a portion of the labor savings could be set aside in a "bonus pot" to be shared by the crew. You would subtract the cost of rework from the labor savings amount to stress the importance of doing it right the first time.

   b. Maintaining a safe work environment with sounds safety practices. If the Foreman and his crew are highly safety-conscious, you may want to add an additional percentage for the safety factor.

   c. Additional dollars could also be set aside for such other critical factors as effective utilization of tools and equipment, attendance and punctuality and working effectively with others.

<u>Example</u>

- Bonus pot is $5,000.00 (% of labor savings minus rework).

- There are 10 eligible people for the bonus, each with a share of $500.00.

- There were positive results in all of the other factors, (safety, equipment, utilization, productivity and teamwork) each with an additional 5% of the bonus share of $500.00. These four additional factors add up to another 20% or an additional $100.00.

- If there are negative results in any of these factors, you would subtract 5% from the bonus pot.

- Maximum bonus opportunity per employee: $600.00

4. Employee Participation

Employee participation—which involves employees in decision-making—gives workers stronger feelings of loyalty to a company. Before making any changes that affect employee performance, it is suggested that you meet with the workers in advance to explain the reasons for the change and to determine if they have any ideas for implementing the change. If you're not going to use the employee's suggestion, then it's important that you explain why.

You could also implement an Action Team approach to improve communications between office and field and to identify barriers that exist in the field that need to be removed to maximize productivity. The Action Team would include several representatives from management and several representatives from the field who would meet every six weeks for one hour (7am-8am) to identify the barriers and discuss solutions for removing them. An agenda is distributed in advance and all participants should come prepared to deal with the issues. At each session, a different manager facilitates the session. The members of the Action Team are rotated every six weeks so that eventually everybody gets involved in the process. The program is based on voluntary participation, so that issues can be dealt with in a positive way. When a solution is suggested, the team is assigned the responsibility for carrying it out. That's where the word "action" comes from. After the meeting, the notes are typed up and distributed to all team members, so they have a record of what went on at the meeting.

5. Positive Reinforcement

This is giving people positive feedback for doing good work. It's the concept of finding somebody dong something right and letting them know you appreciate it. There's a leadership principle that says, "When you reinforce positive behavior, it tends to repeat itself." When giving positive feedback, make sure the following three elements are included:

- Be specific—rather than say "you're quality is good" say the following: "On your last three jobs there was no rework and I want you to know that you have made a positive contribution to the profitability of the job."

- Be timely—the best time to give positive feedback is right away. As you're walking the job and see somebody doing something right, give specific, positive feedback right away—*when you see it, say it*.

- Be relevant—don't just toss compliments around. Make sure you're giving positive feedback for positive actions that enhance the overall success of the job. It's giving feedback to an employee who has improved his/her performance on a specific productivity factor such as safety, teamwork or utilizing tools and equipment effectively.

Positive reinforcement helps make people feel good about themselves which probably will result in their staying with the company.

6. Improving Worker Motivation

There are a variety of things that you can do to facilitate worker motivation and create the desire for people to stay with the company. Here are some of the things you can do:

- Increase pay as an employee's skill improves or when they take on more responsibility.

- Clearly explain what you expect of people and follow up to ensure that they're meeting expectations.

- Provide coaching if they're not sure of how to do something or if they're having difficulty performing an assigned task.

- Remove the barriers that have a negative impact on employee performance and morale.

- Encourage feedback so that negative situations can be dealt with right away.

- Let employees work without interference.

- Give employees all of the resources they need to do their job effectively.

- Provide ongoing feedback on employee performance.

- Let people know how important they are—without them, you couldn't succeed.

All in all, the most important lesson to take away from this chapter is that *the retention of good employees is not a given*. It is up to the employer to make sure the workplace is conducive to employee satisfaction. Retaining good employees leads to a real sense of teamwork. When workers know each other's strengths and weaknesses they establish a willingness to help one another. By having little or no turnover on the job, you also reap the benefits of not having to pay the hidden costs of employee dissatisfaction and poor morale. The challenge: establish and implement a Game Plan for employee retention.

Critical Factor #9

Managing Change

- **The Dynamics of Organizational Change**

The Dynamics of Organizational Change

The companies of today exist in a dynamic and turbulent society in which the question of whether change will occur is no longer relevant. Simply put, change is a given. Societal factors have caused significant change in the work environment, thereby affecting the people, methods and goals of organizations. These modifications occur so quickly that the work force has difficulty maintaining a high level of effectiveness. The factors of continuity and momentum are disrupted and workers are forced to continue on in a game of "catch-up." The frequency and complexity of such elements as advancing technology, government regulations, economic instability, the energy crisis, foreign competition and the changing character of the work force presents enormous pressure for managers in their attempts to keep their organizations current and viable.

So what can we do? First off, let's accept the obvious: Change is a fact of life. Any effective manager must come to terms with this fact. However, they should not just allow change to occur at will. By this I mean they must establish change strategies that help them plan, direct and control. They must acquire the necessary skills to respond effectively to change and maintain a means of survival for their organization.

The purpose of this section is to dig deeper into the question of change and how it affects everyone in the organization. Managers will be provided with the keys to why people resist change, how to overcome that resistance along with guidelines for implementing a plan for change.

It has been said that either the person must change or change will manage the person. Change is indeed inevitable, but differs in frequency and magnitude from situation to situation. Those responsible for effecting meaningful change may feel overwhelmed without the necessary skills and knowledge to cope with it. Becoming aware and learning to use these strategies can increase competence for dealing with change.

Organizational change involves people in that it requires them to change habits, expectations, goals and work activities. People must be managed in new and more responsive ways as time goes on. This is an innovative idea that forces us to conceive, construct and convert our behavior to a new view of organizational reality.

The manager who has the power to create change in an organization is a "change agent." Managers are not hired to maintain the status quo. Instead, they are hired to assist the company and its employees in adapting to the alterations both internal and external. In addition, managers must be activators and executors of the change process.

One of the manager's greatest challenges as a change agent is to produce desirable and meaningful change in an era of complexity. The main role of the change agent is to figure out what should happen and then cause it to happen. The latter part of this mission is the most difficult. To develop and launch plans for change on a meaningful scale, the manager must contribute fundamental qualities of initiative, ingenuity and commitment to the effort.

In the change process, managers will find that people resist change. This resistance is a state of mind that is manifested by active opposition and/or avoidance to the changes at hand.

Twelve Reasons Why People Resist Change

1. They don't understand the purpose for the change.

2. Those affected by the change are not involved in planning for the change.

3. Anxiety about job security.

4. Poor communication.

5. Existing work group relationships are changed.

6. Loyalty becomes the paramount reason for change, not goal achievement.

7. Fear of failure.

8. Work load will intensify.

9. Too much personal sacrifice.

10. Allegiance to work group.

11. Lack of respect for person making change.

12. Comfortable with status quo.

Successful Activation & Execution of Change Encompasses the Ability to…

- Identify, develop or clarify a need for change.

- Explore the readiness and resources for change.

- Define the potential working relationships.

- Negotiate and develop commitment for change.

- Project the desired outcomes of the change effort.

- Plan and design for action.

- Secure appropriate involvement in the change process.

- Implement action and resolve resulting conflicts.

- Analyze and assess.

When Introducing Change—Communicate, Communicate, Communicate!!!

- The reasons for change.

- The benefits the change will bring.

- The rough spots that will be encountered.

- The need for help of everyone involved to implement the change.

The effective manager must have an attitude that constructively questions accepted ways of doing things. They must also have the belief that they can make improvements and a capability to integrate known ideas and techniques into new combinations. Finally, they must have expertise in transferring and applying concepts in various situations, willingness to search beyond the logical and a refusal to waiver in the face of difficulty. These are the "change criteria" that breed excellence and growth, rather than the acceptance of the status quo.

By dealing with change in a positive way, we are at least trying to make things better, rather than sitting around waiting for something to happen. Managing change is being proactive and that is the strategy that will continue to breathe life into the organization and perpetuate success.

Addendum
Productivity Assessment Indicator

Use a Rating Scale of any number between 1-5 for each statement: "1" meaning the activity "hardly ever occurs" and "5" meaning the activity "occurs quite often."

	Activity	Rating
1.	The Foremen set production goals with the crew.	_____
2.	The Foremen track, code and report production daily.	_____
3.	The Foremen maintain adequate manpower on the job.	_____
4.	Foremen have a thorough knowledge of the scope of work, the prints and the quality specs for the job.	_____
5.	Work is done right the first time.	_____
6.	Assigns the right people to the right tasks.	_____
7.	Provides Foremen with a Job Information Packet.	_____
8.	Provides the Foremen with the resources they need when they need them.	_____
9.	Foremen provide positive leadership on the job.	_____
10.	Foremen know how to effectively plan, organize, direct and control.	_____
11.	Foremen provide coaching as required.	_____
12.	Foremen communicate effectively with all of the players in the construction process.	_____
13.	Foremen listen to input from others.	_____
14.	Foremen encourage feedback from their crew.	_____
15.	Pre-Job Planning Meetings are held for all jobs.	_____

16. Foremen do weekly planning. _____

17. Foremen conduct Weekly Tool Box Safety Talks. _____

18. Foremen complete all paperwork accurately and submit on time. _____

19. Foremen review prints before job starts and meet with Estimator to get answers to any questions. _____

20. Foremen hold crew people accountable for substandard performance. _____

21. Foremen know what the productivity standards are for each key job responsibility. _____

22. Foremen follow up and assess the work of the crew and provide coaching as required. _____

23. Foremen document barriers to their productivity. _____

24. Post Job Reviews are conducted when jobs are completed. _____

25. Foremen track, code and report production accurately. _____

FINAL SCORE: _____

Excellent Productivity:	112–125
Good Productivity:	100–111
Fair Productivity:	75–99
Poor Productivity:	less than 75

If your final score is below 100, you should consider doing an Organizational Assessment to identify the barriers to productivity.

Slowikowski & Associates offers such a week-long assessment and will work with your Management Team to establish an Action Plan for improving productivity and maximizing profitability.

To receive complete information on the Organizational Assessment and what it includes, contact Norb Slowikowski:

E-MAIL: **NorbSlow1@aol.com**
PHONE: **(630) 910-8920**
FAX: **(630) 910-8922**

www.making-it-happen.net

978-0-595-39784-6
0-595-39784-0

Printed in the United States
68703LVS00005B/103-189